EVERYDAY
MIRACLES

Encouragement for Everyday Life

By *Shirlee Mooney*

Foreword by Peter Mooney

ISBN 978-1-64299-874-0 (paperback)
ISBN 978-1-64299-875-7 (digital)

Christian Faith Publishing, Inc.
832 Park Avenue
Meadville, PA 16335
www.christianfaithpublishing.com

Printed in the United States of America

This book is dedicated to God, who has the
power to perform daily miracles.
To my kids, Peter and Dianna, and my loving husband,
Steve, who have traveled the journey with me.

ACKNOWLEDGMENT

Many thanks to my early editors, Peter and Joy, who encouraged me through this process and Dianna for working on the illustrations. Also much thanks for the emotional support and love from my husband Steve. I also want to thank all my friends and family who were a part of these stories and for allowing me to share God's miracles with the world. Finally, special thanks to Faith Christian Publishing Co. for believing in me.

FOREWORD

Shirlee, my mother, has been a great inspiration to me for as long as I can remember. She is a very passionate individual with an enthusiasm for life and God that is the envy of all who meet her. Her always cheerful demeanor has brightened many a dark time and lifted countless spirits. This same pizzazz carries over into her writing as the majority of the topics deal with those things most important to her: faith, family, and friends. Many of the stories in this book come directly out of her life experiences and it's enlightening to see from her perspective the exact same events that I remember growing up.

When she approached me with the idea for this book, I was hesitant at first and doubted that she would actually follow through on committing to it. I am glad to say she has proven me wrong yet again. Throughout the whole process, I have done my best to support her with encouragement and basic editing. It's exciting to see the project come this far, and it will be equally exciting to see where things go from here. I know God has special plans for her and for this book. We will all be praying for your continued success and God's blessing in your life.

Best of luck, Mom!

Peter Mooney

I Can't Give Up My Only Son!

"For God so loved the world that he gave his one and only Son, that whosoever believes in Him shall not perish but have eternal life."

—John 3:16

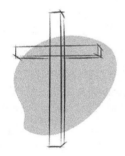

Peter, my one and only son, lay quietly on the hospital bed. Something was terribly wrong with him. "Quiet" was not in his vocabulary. Energetic, smart, fun, intense, and extremely active were good words to describe my ten-year-old, but not quiet. He could hardly move or talk, let alone breathe. What was going on with him? I approached his nurse and asked if an oxygen saturation test could be done on him as I was concerned about his breathing. Being a nurse, I had some knowledge about tests and bloodwork. But being a mother, my feelings took over. The nurse said, "He is just fine. We have him on antibiotics. He just needs rest."

I tried to keep calm and said, "This is not like my son, something is wrong. I know my son."

She said she needed an order and the doctor was at a Christmas party, and she didn't want to disturb him. As Peter's lips became more bluish in color, I cried out to God, "Please, God, don't take my one and only son. I know you gave up your only Son, but I just can't do that. He is so young. I know you have great plans ahead for him. Please, God, I beg you don't let him die!"

It was around 9:00 p.m. when a respiratory worker strolled into the hospital room to check the child in the next bed. When he had finished, I asked him if he could just put the finger monitor on Peter to check his oxygen, and he gladly agreed to do that. He repeated it three times and said, "His oxygen is 84 percent and should be in the 90 percent range." He ran to the nurse's station, and before you could blink an eye, oxygen was placed on Peter and all kinds of activity began. They took X-rays of his lungs and ran blood tests and the doctor appeared shortly after. The next thing I knew, Peter was being transferred to the intensive care unit. He had double pneumonia. The doctor stayed and checked on him repeatedly during the night. Peter slowly began to move around and talk. He would recover. I then called to update my sister. She said she had such a burden for Peter that she began praying intensely around 9:00 p.m. I couldn't believe it.

Prayer: *"Dear Father, thank you for loving me so much that you gave up your one and only Son, Jesus, for me. Thank you that you spared my son Peter from dying so young and for answered prayers. I am excited to see what great things you have in store for him."*

Do I Have to Go?

"For the Lord God is a sun and shield: the Lord bestows favor and honor; no good thing does he withhold from those whose walk is blameless."

—Psalms 64:11

It was a beautiful sunny and warm Saturday in Minnesota, and I wanted to get out of the house to go to the garage sales that were being held in town. I asked my husband, Steve, to go with me. He had just gotten back from a business trip the night before, and I had missed him and had lots of things I wanted to share with him. He replied, "Do I have to go? I never find anything for myself." He immediately noted my frown and said, "But it will be great to get outside and walk and spend time with you." I gave him a big hug and thanked him. As we were holding hands and walking, I silently prayed, "God, could you please help us find some things for my hubby. I want him to relax and have fun today. He works so hard, please bless him today."

The first garage sale had lots of beautiful dresses, women's clothing, and purses. I was excited! However, there was nothing there that interested Steve. I purchased a few items, and we walked next door to the next sale. Steve spotted a tennis racket that was a good brand, in excellent condition, and the price was cheap. He bought it on the spot. I thanked God and enjoyed watching Steve beam about the deal he had just got. We continued on to the next home where Steve went to the men's stuff while I headed to the jewelry table. The next thing I noticed was Steve smiling and holding a fishing pole he had just bought. I smiled and thanked God again.

We continued to proceed from yard to yard while laughing, sharing, and enjoying each other. It was soon 11:30 a.m., and we were getting hungry for a quick snack and were delighted when the next home had candy bars for sale. We love candy, but we had been trying to lose weight and were cutting down on our sugar consumption. I mentioned it to the man that was selling the candy bars, and he said he had a box of sugar-free chocolate bars in the house that we could have. He brought them out, and I could not believe it: they were Steve's favorite candy bar! As we ended our day, I could contain my joy no longer. I shared with Steve how I prayed that he would have a great day and how I asked God to bless him. He admitted he had a wonderful time and said, "Let's go again soon."

Prayer: *"Dear Father, thank you for blessing me with a godly husband and pouring your favor on him. Thank you for answered prayers and knowing our wants and giving us more than we deserve. You are so amazing!"*

What a Surprise!

"My times are in your hands."

—Psalms 31:15

I was excited to head to California to visit my daughter and son-in-law. It had been a long winter, full of cold and snow. I looked forward to the warm sunshine and visiting with the kids. My husband had to work and airline tickets were pricey this time of year. I usually fly into Burbank, which is ten minutes away from them, but Los Angeles was over $150 cheaper. So today I was going to fly into Los Angeles. Just as much as I love the warm weather of Los Angeles, I despise the traffic. I didn't look forward to having the kids drive to pick me up at the Los Angeles airport. My daughter had joked with me on my last trip and said, "Just close your eyes and don't jump while I drive. You make me crazy. You just have to go with the flow, Mom." The Los Angeles traffic, with its eight lanes, had indeed made me crazy at times! I had prayed for cheap tickets to Burbank months ago, but God had said no. So here I was heading to Los Angeles.

My flight left Grand Rapids and stopped over in Minnesota. I got my Caribou Coffee and found my next connection. I sat down and started reading a book I had brought with me. Then I heard the airline representative say, "We have overbooked. Would anyone be willing to take a later flight to California?" I jumped up and ran to the ticket counter. I could take a later flight! In exchange, the airline would give me a $400 flight voucher and a dinner voucher as a gift. It would also mean a four-hour delay in Minnesota. That would be fine with me as I would have to wait in LA till my daughter got out of work anyway. Then a thought hit me: the Holy Spirit was nudging me! So I shyly asked if it was possible to fly into Burbank instead of LA. The airline rep pushed a few keys on the computer and said, "No problem. Plus, that flight leaves in two hours instead of four."

What a pleasant surprise God gave me that day. I thought He had said "no" to my prayer request months earlier when He had actually said, "Wait." God's timing had been perfect.

Prayer: *"Dear Father, my times are in your hands. Your answers to my prayers are never too early and never too late. Thank you, God, for the wonderful surprise of a free airline voucher, a delicious dinner, and flying directly into Burbank. You are awesome!"*

Exercise? Forget it!

"Do you not know your body is a temple of the Holy Spirit, who is in you, whom you have received from God? You are not your own: you were bought at a price. Therefore, honor God with your body."

—1 Corinthians 6:19

 I was shocked and very disappointed when I learned Curves, my exercise place, was going to close down. I had been going to Curves at least three times a week for the past seven years. I had my routine, and it fit in nicely with my busy schedule. I had met many wonderful and supportive ladies there and was sad it was shutting down.

I prayed about finding a place to exercise and then decided I could do it on my own. Right! Three weeks later, I had gained three pounds and felt stiff all over. I knew I needed help. It was then I became mad and asked God why Curves closed down. I continued to spiral to an all-time low. It was Christmastime, and I felt sorry for myself. I had gained weight, felt sluggish, and found out I would have to spend Christmas day all alone since my husband had to work and the kids were out of town. I really blew it: I had cake, chips, cookies, and anything my eyes delighted in. I just didn't care. I felt like nobody loved me or cared about me. So why should I?

As I read my devotions that morning, the Holy Spirit began a work in my soul. God cared and loved me so much that he gave

His son, Jesus, for me. I broke down and sobbed and submitted my appetite and body to him. I prayed for help in finding another place to exercise and began looking the next day. I found Planet Fitness. What a joy to discover that they had more than I could image. It had trainers, workout machines, treadmills, weights, TVs, music, massage beds and chairs, and even tanning beds! I also saw two friends from my old gym. Planet Fitness was having a special that day and the price was one-half of what I had been paying for Curves. I guess I would exercise and take care of my body; it certainly made me feel better, plus God had spoken. God had provided me again with more than I could have dreamed.

Prayer: *"Dear Father, thank you for providing a place to take care of my body, where your Spirit dwells. Thank you for paying the price for it with Jesus. Thank you for loving me more than I deserve. Help me take care of my body for you."*

Angel in the Junk Yard

"Even though I walk through the valley of the shadow of death,
I will fear no evil, for you are with me; your rod and your staff,
they comfort me."

—Psalm 23:4

I needed a plastic drawer for my refrigerator, one that holds the lettuce and fresh vegetables. Mine broke and was no longer usable. I looked up the replacement cost on the internet and was horrified to find out it cost eighty-four dollars. How could a plastic drawer cost that much? I went to prayer and asked God to provide one that was cheap and fit my refrigerator, as there are many different sizes and styles.

I called around and could not find one. I spoke with a friend, Barb, who suggested I look at a "Re-Store." This is a place where people donate building supplies, stoves, refrigerators, parts, etc. Then the store sells the donated merchandise inexpensively. I went to the Re-Store and continued to pray that my need would be met. I had no luck, but an employee suggested I go across the street to the junkyard. My heart started to race, as I am terrified of rats and mice and knew I could not go through the junkyard without freaking out. "God," I prayed, "You must be mistaken!" But I knew in my heart I had to go to the junkyard. God would be with me and comfort me and I had to trust Him. I could not let my fear stop me from obeying His voice. I had to do it even though I was afraid.

I went across the street to the junkyard and checked in at the office. I was directed to pile no. 3 and told to be careful as I searched through the junk. My heart began racing even faster; my palms were sweaty, and I felt like I was going to die! I was praying like crazy for strength and willpower. As I was about to step into the pile and begin my search, a man stepped out from behind the huge pile and asked, "May I help you?" I explained that I was looking for a plastic drawer for my refrigerator. The employee smiled and said, "I just pulled two of them out this morning and put them to the side. What size do you need?" I told him and he had my size drawer. I didn't have to go in the junk with the mice and rats. I praised God for being with me and providing an angel to rescue me. Overjoyed, I went to pay for the plastic drawer. I then learned you pay for an item by the weight. The total cost came to one dollar and fifty-eight cents . . . I couldn't believe it!

God had answered my prayer. I could trust Him to be with me, to send His angel and to comfort me, even when I was afraid.

Prayer: *"Dear Father, help me to always trust you, even when I am afraid."*

Tears

"I waited patiently for the Lord: He turned to me and heard my cry."

—Psalm 40:1

How could my friend be so wrong? She was supposed to support me and know my heart and motives. I could not believe the words she just spoke. She said I was being selfish, inflexible, and demanding. It felt like a brick fell on my head. I burst out crying and could not even speak. I was sobbing so hard I had to run from her house. I drove home in tears. I cried out to God, "Help me, Lord. You know my heart and motives. Please show me how to handle this situation." I cried for the next week. Finally, there were no more tears, and I asked God to use these hurting accusations to make the truth known.

In the following weeks, God's Word comforted me and showed me the truth. Hurting people hurt others. What could possibly be hurting my friend to cause her to lash out about the past ten years? All that time she had been holding grudges, and I had thought everything was wonderful. God began to reveal to me many things as I sought Him in prayer and Bible study. I began to see my own faults and sins, and it was not pretty. The truth began to unravel. But I also saw how much God loved me and gave me His gift of forgiveness and grace. I needed to love my friend and forgive her, just as God had done for me. God had given up his only Son for me. Surely through God's power, I could give up some of my selfish ways for my friend. Yes, it did hurt and I still had moments of anger at being misunderstood. But through God, I would persevere and not give up on our relationship. It would be hard, but worth it in the end. God had heard my prayer and cry. With God's help, our relationship would not only survive but grow.

Prayer: *"Dear Father, thank you for loving me so much that You gave up Your Son, Jesus, for me. Thank you for hearing my cries and wiping away all my tears. Thank you for the strength to forgive and love my friend and not to just give up on her, and run away from our relationship."*

Disappointment Turns to Joy

"Weeping may endure for a night but Joy comes in the morning."

—Psalm 30:5

I was excited as I packed my suitcase for my upcoming business cruise. Only one week away. I could picture myself sitting on the balcony of my room enjoying each morning. I would be looking at the beautiful massive ocean, coffee, and Bible in hand, enjoying the warm breeze. What a great way to worship my God and Savior. Being a hospice nurse and having a busy life, I could already feel the peace and beauty that would surround me on that balcony. I continued to ponder these thoughts when the phone rang bringing me back to reality. My sister, Barb, called to say we didn't get a balcony room. We got an inside room with no window. The ship was full, and we were stuck in the windowless room with no balcony. I couldn't believe it; I wanted to cry. I had been looking forward to my quiet, peaceful mornings with God and his beautiful creation for weeks. As I hung up the phone, I thought, "I don't get it! Why, God, why? I don't understand, don't you love and value me, asking for a balcony isn't too much to ask, is it?" I was very disappointed and sad. I finished packing and happened to glance outside. It was getting dark, snowing heavily and the thermometer in the window said twenty-one degrees. I would try to focus on the blessings of warmer weather on my cruise and forget about not getting a balcony room. I tried, but I failed. I talked to my husband who said, "It could be worse." My emotions went from disappointment to pity. Doesn't God care about me? Doesn't He love and value me? I don't deserve His favor and blessings. Satan had a great time lying to me, and I took the bait. Finally, I burst into tears and went to bed very disappointed.

The next morning when I woke up, I confessed my bad attitude to God and believed He knew what was best for me. The rest of the week went by quickly, and before I knew it, I was boarding the cruise ship with my sister, Barb. We were in line and got handed our documents, which said "VIP" on them. I asked a cruise representative what that meant and she said I was a very important person and to follow her. We skipped by the hundreds of people waiting in line and went into a small room where we got registered right away. I was given a platinum fun card. I was told I would have many benefits— free spa treatments, chocolate-covered fruit and goodies delivered to our room, free laundry and immediate service, no standing in lines. Wow, I could not believe it. My heart was overwhelmed with joy. My sister said, "God's favor is on you and I get to go along for the ride. Cool!" It was the start of a fun-filled cruise with a God who did love me. That surprising miracle turned into a lifelong lesson for me. I was His VIP. He had loved me so much He gave his only Son, Jesus, and I was valued and important to Him. Why had I doubted His love? I did matter! He had turned my disappointment into unbelievable joy.

Prayer: *"Dear Father, thank you for loving and valuing me so much. Thank you for Your Son, Jesus, who made it all possible."*

God Will Guide Me

*"I will instruct you and teach you in the way to go.
I will guide you with my eye."*

—Psalm 32:8

Listening hasn't always been my greatest skill. I am more of a talker, and I love to get my words in on a daily basis. But the times I have concentrated on listening, I have always been rewarded. One time, in particular, comes to mind. The time I woke up on a Tuesday morning at 5:00 a.m. After tossing and turning and not being able to go back to sleep, I reluctantly dragged myself out of my warm bed. I decided to enjoy a nice, long, quiet time with God. I would pray, read my devotions, and mediate. I have always enjoyed my peaceful and quiet mornings. A time just for God and me.

My mind was full with concerns that morning; my full-time job as a nurse at Hospice, my kids, and my husband's health. No matter how tired I was, I knew from past experience that I always felt refreshed and energized after spending time with the Lord. I was sitting on the sofa all bundled up with Bently, my dog, by my side. I had my Bible and coffee in hand and was ready to begin enjoying my relationship with my personal Savior. I listened as the Holy Spirit spoke to me that morning and the message was clear. Psalm 32:8

said, *"I will instruct you and teach you in the way to go. I will guide you with my eye."*

God would help me, lead me, and guide me, but I had to listen. I invited him in my life to guide my every moment and prayed that I would be more aware of Him on a daily basis. I prayed I would be in tune with His voice, His inner nudging, every minute of the day. I prayed I would really listen to His will and have the courage to obey, whether it made sense to me or not. I have always struggled with wanting to see the entire puzzle and not just one piece at a time. I guess that is where faith comes in. I needed to learn to trust Him one piece of my life at a time.

As I finished my time with the Lord, I felt revived, ready to start my day. I got dressed for work, praising God for His promise to guide me. I was ready to listen and obey. I hopped in the car and made my way to work. As I was pulling into the parking lot, I heard the Holy Spirit (inner nudging) say, "Don't park where you usually park. Park on the opposite side of the parking lot." I obeyed and pulled into a distant spot.

At my desk, I began to plan the day. I would finish charting, call and confirm my home visits, and meet with my boss. Around 9:00 a.m. an announcement came over the loudspeaker, "There has been an accident in the front parking lot, and four cars have been hit. Please proceed to the parking lot if you own one of the following cars." The announcer then continued to list the type of cars that were involved in the accident. My car, a Buick, was not included in the list. I was so thankful!

Shortly afterward, I found out what had happened. A man had been speeding and couldn't make the corner. He flew into our parking lot and collided with four parked cars. Alcohol was most likely a factor in the accident. One of the cars was completely totaled and the other three were slightly damaged. The totaled car was located exactly where I would normally park mine. I could not believe it! It was a miracle and a powerful lesson for me. God would Guide me, all I needed to do was listen and obey.

Prayer: *"Dear Father, thank you for the promise of Your word to guide me and teach me. Help me to listen and obey even when I don't know why."*

God Will Provide

"God will meet all your needs, according to
His glorious riches in Christ Jesus."

—Philippians 4:19

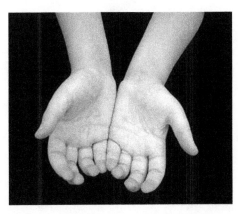

It was a great day to take my dog, Bently, for a walk. I stepped outside to begin my journey and the wind rustled through my hair. I smiled. At that moment, all was good.

About fifteen minutes into the walk I noticed Bently giving me all the signs that he was about to "go to the bathroom." Instantly, I realized I had forgotten to bring a plastic "doo doo" bag. I try to be conscientious and was embarrassed to think that I would not be able to clean up after my dog. "God," I pleaded, "please, help Bently not go, not here, not now." Bently continued squirming, and in an effort to avoid my dilemma, I picked up my pace and almost fell over him. I cried out to God again in my mind. "Please, God, help him wait."

Just then, a proverb sprung into my mind:

"When people can't see what God is doing, they stumble all over themselves: but when they attend to what He reveals they are most blessed."

I looked up and saw a white plastic bag blow across the road and land at my feet. I picked up the bag, Bently did his job, and I continued on my walk, amazed at God's provision. My prayer had not been answered like I had requested, but God had provided a better way. That simple miracle turned into a powerful lesson for me: God will provide for my needs, even if it is not in the way I expected.

Prayer: *"Dear Heavenly Father, help me to open my eyes and see all the ways You provide for me."*

Sunglasses

"Are not two sparrows sold for a penny? Yet not one of them will fall to the ground apart from the will of your Father. And even the very hairs of your head are all numbered. So don't be afraid; you are worth more than many sparrows."

—Matthew 10:29–31

"You need to consider quitting your job," my husband, Steve, told me. I was mad! I loved my job and it helped us live a comfortable lifestyle. Oh, I knew we had some concerns about the direction that our sixteen-year-old daughter was heading. And, yes, I knew she needed more monitoring. We had just had a fight the past weekend and had caught her drinking. But, God, why do I have to quit my job? After several days of intense prayer and heated discussion with God, I could take it no longer and knew I had to obey Him and resign. What was more important, family or things? Steve provided enough to take care of us and God had always come through in the past.

As I was driving home from work on the last day, I was still whining to God. "I just don't understand, God, it was the ideal job! This job had good hours, great pay, and You know how I lose my sunglasses every summer. How can I possibly afford to buy multiple pairs of sunglasses?" The year before, I had gone through three pairs of sunglasses. I dropped one off the boat, left a pair in a restaurant, and stepped on and broke another. "God, I know this seems small," I thought, "but do you really care?"

I was almost home when I spotted a yard sale and stopped. To my surprise, I spotted a pink plastic basin filled with new sunglasses, which still had price tags on them. "How much are these sunglasses?" I asked. The elderly man said, "Take the whole basin for one dollar." I bought them and proceeded directly to my car and began to cry uncontrollably. God did care—even about the small things! He loved me and would take care of me.

Prayer: *"Dear Father, Forgive me when I rebel against Your will for me. Thank you for showing me how much You love me and take care of me even when I am afraid and rebel."*

Out Give God, I Dare You!

"Bring the whole tithe into the storehouse, that there may be food in my house. Test me in this, says the Lord Almighty, and see if I will not throw open the floodgates of heaven and pour out so much blessing that you will not have room enough for it."

—Malachi 3:11

My husband and I have a "God Can." We put extra money in it when we have some. It is supposed to be used for fun or blessing others whom God lays on our hearts. I can be selfish at times and justify that I need something and help myself to it. For example, I love Yankee candles. They are expensive, but they do a great job of setting the atmosphere when we entertain. We are commanded to be hospitable, right? My last candle had burned out and I wanted a replacement. I also had been thrifty and purchased a "made in Italy," high count thread, sheet set from a yard sale. The green sheets were so soft and beautiful and nearly new. Now I wanted to purchase two matching pillowcases, but they were very expensive. Could I justify getting them for my overnight guests? I was debating these thoughts when I heard a "beep."

Just then, I received a text message from my husband stating we should take out some friends for lunch on his day off. Could I check the "God Can" to see how much is in it and call to see if our friends are available? He also said he wanted to take them somewhere nice to eat and help them feel appreciated and encouraged. We had prayed about them that morning and many days before, and I thought it was a great idea. But then I struggled about my desires and wants (candle and pillowcases). I had to confess to God that although my desires weren't wrong, maybe the timing wasn't the best. A verse in Malachi came to my mind, something about trying to out give God and I decided I would try to do that.

The following Monday, we took our friends to a very nice restaurant and showered them with love and kind words. We encouraged them to keep on in their ministry for the Lord and not to give up. I was on cloud nine seeing hope in their faces once again.

The next day, I went to work. I work at a second-hand store as a clerk. I was putting away baskets of dishes, clothes, toys, hardware, etc. I could not believe it when right before my eyes I saw a brand-new Yankee candle for forty-nine cents. It was one of my favorite scents, lavender. I praised God and continued working. When I got down to the bottom of the baskets, I saw two pillowcases that matched my green sheets, and it was the exact same brand, the pillowcases were priced at ninety-nine cents. This time, I let out a scream of joy. My co-worker hurried over, asking me what had happened. I explained to her about the "God Can" and how God had dared me, through the Bible, to "out give" Him. This indeed was a miracle for me. He again showed me how much He loves and cares for me and that there is "no way" I could ever out give Him.

Prayer: *"Thank you for providing for me again and again. Your Word is true and so powerful. Thank you for the many blessings you have given me!"*

Obedience Is the Key

"Does the Lord delight in burnt offerings and sacrifices as much as in obeying the voice of the Lord? To obey is better than sacrifices and to heed is better than the fat of rams."

—1 Samuel 15:22–23

I was stressed, so much to do and so little time. My husband had been traveling all week and the majority of responsibilities fell on me. We were planning on leaving for our much-anticipated vacation on Sunday to a warmer climate. It was the middle of February on Saturday, and I still had to finish packing, check on the kids' suitcases, do last-minute laundry, plus take the dog to its sitter. I also hoped to run to the local mall and get a pair of white sandals that would go perfectly with my outfits. That morning, as I had my time with God, the Holy Spirit spoke to me and impressed on my heart what I needed to do. God was asking me to trust him and honor my husband by spending a few hours with him and doing what he wanted to do. Steve had a stressful week and wanted to go snowmobiling for a while, as this really relaxes him. My first thought was, "You have got to be kidding, God. I have no time for that!" But after prayer and reading my Bible, I knew what I had to do. I had to obey God. I prayed God would give me a joyful attitude, go snowmobiling, and trust Him for the rest.

Later that morning, as we got on the snowmobile and headed into the woods, I realized it was going to be a magical day. The sun was shining, the snow was crystal clean, and the wooded paths were well groomed. God had changed my attitude and agenda, and I was honestly excited to go snowmobiling. We laughed as we took off like two silly teenagers without a care in the world. After about two hours, we came across a small cafe and my husband suggested that we stop and get a cup of coffee and a doughnut. I agreed. We had a delightful time as he poured out his heart and shared with me what had been happening the past week. He said how thankful he was that I was willing to flex my plans and go out with him. As we were about to leave, the waitress came to us and said she also had a store in the back where she was selling her merchandise at 75 percent off. Did we want to take a look? "Sure," I said and headed to the store area. To my surprise, there was a pair of cute white sandals, marked down to three dollars. They were a size 6, just my size. I could not believe it! I tried them on and they fit perfectly and they were so cute and comfortable. Who but God could have brought us to this little cafe, in the middle of the desolate woods in the Upper Peninsula of Michigan?

Needless to say, my clothes got washed, my packing got done, the dog got to the sitter, and we even got to bed at a decent time. And I had been blessed with a wonderful, joyful, sunny day, an appreciative hubby and a pair of white sandals. Obedience was the key!

Prayer: *"Dear Father, Help me to always obey You even when my flesh doesn't want to. You love me and have the best plans for my life. Help me to trust and obey You every day."*

I Am Running Away!

"The Lord himself goes before you and will be with you; he will never leave you nor forsake you. Do not be afraid; do not be discouraged."

—Deuteronomy 31:8

I was hurt and mad at my friend, at God, and at the way my life was turning out. I had enough of disappointments and failures in my life. I was giving up and going to run away from God, my faith, and responsibilities. I was going to be free and do exactly what I wanted to do when I wanted to do it, with no strings attached. I put on my jogging shoes and said to God, "This is it! I am running away from you. My life just hurts too much, and I can't take it anymore. I am out of here." With that said, I headed out the door to go on my three-mile run.

The fresh warm air felt good on my face as I picked up my pace and got my rhythm going. About five minutes into my run, a rabbit ran in front of me. I immediately thought about God and creation. I continued to run, and as I turned the corner in the woods, a beautiful deer with big brown eyes was standing on the side of the path about ten feet in front of me. Again, I thought about God, the Creator of life. My heart began to soften as I observed the trees, the leaves, and the sun shining through them. Who else but God could create such beauty? I could hear the birds chirp and the noisy running of the squirrels. They were taken care of and didn't worry or fret.

Near the end of my run, the tears started to flow, how could I run away from God, He was everywhere. Why would I run away from God, when He was the only person who could give me true freedom and life? He took care of the animals and would take care of me. I decided to run to Him and prayed for His help. I surrendered my disappointments, my problems, and my will to Him. He did care!

Prayer: *"Dear Father, thank you for never leaving me. Forgive me when I run away from You, thinking I can do life better. Thank you for encouraging me on my daily journey and always going with me!"*

Pray about That?

"Ask and it will be given you: seek and you will find,
knock and the door will be opened to you."

—Matthew 7:7

My husband, Steve, and I were working on a rental house. It was almost complete and ready for the new residents to move in. We were tired and ready to be finished with working on it. A few more minutes and we would be done. Yes, I could hardly wait! As we were putting up the last blind in the dining room window, the plastic tip broke off, and I snapped. Why did this happen now? I had places to go, and things to do and this did not need to happen! I would have to run to Menards and get a new blind, which would take at least an hour and I didn't have the time nor the mind-set to do this. I would also have to purchase a completely new blind, which was costly, and we had already gone over our estimated budget. Why, God, why now? Can't anything ever go smoothly? Needless to say, I was discouraged.

Just this morning in my devotions, I had prayed for God's will to be done with the rental and to honor him with our business, Heavenly Dwellings, LLC. I just didn't understand how God could use this in my life. I had prayed to become close to God and worship

Him on a moment to moment basis. Sensing my frustration, Steve said a quick prayer before I headed to Menards. He prayed something about getting in and out of the store quickly, finding the right size blind, and it being on sale. *Yea, right*, I thought. My attitude definitely needed improving.

As I went into Menards, I went right to the window treatment section and saw a clerk. I explained what had happened, and he got a big grin on his face. He reached down into a pile of broken blinds and pulled off the tip that I needed. I was shocked. "How much?" I asked.

"Nothing," he said, "I was going to throw these away, and you came just in time."

I thanked him and skipped to my car, thanking God for answered prayer. I could hardly wait to get back to the rental home and share with Steve about God's goodness, answered prayer, and His perfect timing.

Prayer: *"Dear Father, thank You for Your Word, and keeping Your promises. Help me to always ask and seek Your will for my life—especially in the daily events. Thank you for answered prayers and Your eternal love for me."*

Throw Some Stones

*"Let him who is without sin among you be
the first to throw a stone at her."*

—John 8:7

I was working as a visiting nurse in
Florida and loved 90 percent of my job.
I had been praying for my co-workers to
find the Lord and that God would help me
make a difference in their lives. But that
particular Wednesday, as I was in the office
charting, I could hold my tongue no longer. "Lord, help me take a stand, this is not
right," I prayed. Finally, I got the courage to speak. "That's pure gos-
sip," I said to my three co-workers as they were talking about another
nurse named Janet. Janet was not there and could not defend herself.
She was out on a home visit and rumors were going around the office
like wildfire about her. "She is lazy and mean to her patients!" said
one.

"She thinks she is better and smarter than anyone else!" said
another.

"I think she is having an affair with a doctor," whispered another.

I had heard enough! Finally, I said, "Are any one of us perfect?
Maybe we should do what they did in the biblical days and throw
stones at her until she dies. The first person without any sin in their
lives gets to throw the first stone." With that said, I picked up my

paperwork and said I had to go make a visit. Everyone just looked at me with their mouths open. I hardly ever say anything, so I think they got the hint that I was upset.

The next morning, as I came into the office and sat at my desk, I noticed a jar with stones in it. My three co-workers started laughing at me when I saw the jar. They admitted they may have been a little hard on Janet, but swore they knew some of the things were true. They didn't mean anything, they were just venting.

I must admit I was hurt by the jar on the desk implying that I was without sin and perfect, but I trusted God to use me to be a witness for Him. Two of my co-workers had visits to make and left, and only Terry remained in the office with me. She then began to ask all about the Bible and sin. I was able to share with her about God's forgiveness and love. She said she knew I was different from the other girls and that she had been searching for a "change." I wish I could have led her to know Christ personally that day, but I didn't. It was four months later that she walked into the office and said, "I found the Lord this weekend, and I am done throwing stones."

Prayer: *"Dear Father, thank you for being with me when life throws rocks at me and I hurt. Thanks for Your forgiveness and love and for saving my friend, Terry!"*

We Are Out of Cat Food

"Be ye angry, and sin not: Let not the sun go down upon your wrath."

—Ephesians 4:26

I had a very hectic, busy day. It consisted of menu planning, grocery shopping, paying bills, cooking, laundry, and getting up early to get bloodwork drawn. My dog, Bently, got his hair cut and nails trimmed and then I had Bible study at my home at 5:30 p.m. I was spiritually fulfilled but exhausted physically. Finally, I could put my feet up in the recliner, have my cherry Coke, watch TV, and relax.

Just then, my husband yells from the kitchen, "We are out of cat food." My mind went crazy with thoughts of killing him. He knows we have a list to write down items we are out of. He knew I was grocery shopping today, and he knew the bag was low yesterday. My spiritual day was about to get very ugly. He feeds the cat, as one of his jobs. A thousand words crossed my mind and they weren't pretty. But instead, I silently prayed, "Help me, Jesus, right now! Help me not say what I am thinking."

I was not going to let Satan steal my joy and victorious day because we were out of cat food. Instead, through the Holy Spirit's help, I said, "Please write it down on the list and I will try to get it tomorrow."

My husband came into the room and said, "Sorry, honey, I know you went to the store today. I know I don't tell you enough, but I really do appreciate all you do around here." I smiled to myself, thanking God for the victory! I pictured Satan sneaking away with an empty bag of cat food . . . totally defeated.

Prayer: *"Dear Father, thank you for helping me hold my anger and not sin by saying unkind words to my wonderful, but sometimes forgetful, husband. Thank you for helping me defeat Satan and for providing a victorious day!"*

Rescued

"Do not be afraid, I will save you. I have called you by name, you are mine. When you pass through deep waters, I will be with you: your troubles will not overwhelm you. When you pass through fire, you will not be burned: the hard trials that come will not hurt you. For I am the Lord your God, the holy God of Israel, who saves you."

—Isaiah 43:1–3

Steve, my husband; Peter, my son; his wife, Marie; my four-year-old grandson, Pierce; and I were enjoying a nice Sunday afternoon. We had just finished eating at a local restaurant and were headed to our boat to go for a ride. Sunshine, warm temperatures, family, and a boat ride on Lake Michigan make for one happy Mama.

We hopped in and off we flew over the waves into Muskegon Lake headed to the channel, which would take us into Lake Michigan. The channel is a no-wake zone so we slowed down. About halfway through the channel, our boat stopped. We couldn't understand why. Then we discovered we were out of gas. I began to panic internally. Pierce could not swim; what if we tipped over? Would the life jacket keep him afloat? Wild thoughts ran through my mind. Just then, walking by the channel, I saw my sister and her husband. I could not believe it; I had not even had time to pray! God was watching over us. We yelled to them and my brother-in-law "just happened" to have a gallon of gas in his garage, which was a quick five-minute walk around the corner. He ran to get it, we put it in the boat, and off we went. We thanked God for rescuing us and providing a miracle once again.

Prayer: *"Dear Father, thank you for rescuing me and my family from what could have been a boating disaster. Thank you for knowing my needs even before I ask. You are my life savior and I love you so much."*

Surprised by an Unexpected Blessing

"Be imitators of God, therefore, as dearly loved children and live a life of love, just as Christ loved us and gave himself up for us as a fragrant offering and sacrifice to God."

—Ephesians 5:1–2

I was working part-time at a second-hand store and loved it. It was a ministry more than a job to me. People came and went, opened up their hearts to me, and I regularly prayed for their needs and desires. Many of the folks were financially strapped due to loss of jobs, divorce, or foolish spending. They really struggled from paycheck to paycheck. I felt especially blessed on that Thursday morning. My bills were all paid up, groceries bought for the week, and I even had "fun money" and "ministry money" in my God container. I had no financial needs at that moment and was truly praising God for his provision as I heard about so many needs from customers.

Just then, a regular customer, Jody, walked into the store. She grabbed my hand and slipped something into it. Jody was an elderly Christian who loved the Lord but often had to use her pennies to make purchases. In spite of her struggles, she was always positive and showed such faith. She often told me stories about how God always provided for her. I knew she had no husband. She was living on a small social security check and had difficulties meeting her monthly budget. She had a beautiful smile on her face and glowed when she said to me, "I love you and God told me to bless you today and so don't refuse my gift." She then hugged me and immediately departed out of the store. As I opened my hand, I saw $25. I was shocked and upset because I knew she had so many needs. I asked God, why? I had plenty; I didn't need it at that time. Then the Holy Spirit brought a thought to my mind, maybe Jody needed to give and sacrifice to God for her growth. I could not argue with God working in Jody's life, so I would keep the money even when it was difficult for me to do so. What an example to me she was in sacrificial giving. I knew I needed to do more of it and be a blessing to others. She had shown me how to be like Jesus and I would imitate Him too!

Prayer: *"Dear Father, thank you for an unexpected blessing of money and for a lesson learned on sacrificial giving. Please bless my friend for obeying You and showing me how to truly love and give to others."*

It Is a Dead Minnow

"We have different gifts according to the grace given us. If the gift is encouragement, let him encourage, if it is contributing to the needs of others, let him give generously, if it is leadership let him govern diligently, if it is showing mercy, let him do it cheerfully."

—Romans 12:6–8

I love to fish and I love to eat fish. That is why I was so excited when I found a brooch that was made from a dead minnow. It was a conversation piece, to say the least. I remember that Wednesday morning, as I got up and attached my minnow pin to my pink shirt, it looked so good!

I was studying the gifts of the spirit for my devotional time. As I studied the gifts of the spirit, I began to realize that I had the gift of encouraging others and giving. At the conclusion of my devotions that morning, I prayed, "Use me today, Lord, to give and to encourage others." I knew I had a busy day planned and things to do. I had to grocery shop, go to Bible study, and have coffee with a hurting friend. I was excited to see how God would work in my day to answer my prayer.

I started the day with grocery shopping and got everything but the fish I wanted. I decided I had time to stop at the fish market. As I was picking out my walleye, the clerk noted the minnow pin on my shirt. She said, "I love that pin, where did you get it? It would be perfect for me working here." I told her that it was one of a kind that I found at a yard sale the year before. Her excited face became sad as she said, "Oh." The Holy Spirit then nudged me to take it off and hand it to her. I would like to tell you that I listened to the Holy Spirit and obeyed, but I didn't! I loved my very unique minnow pin, so I paid for my walleye and left the store.

As soon as I got in the car and drove away, I realized I had missed the blessing of giving and encouraging that clerk at the fish store. I argued with myself, "It is only a dead minnow preserved in a plastic coating and put on a pin. It's no big deal if the clerk gets it or not." I then continued with my other errands.

The day flew by, and before I knew it, I was home and getting ready for bed. As I took my minnow pin off my shirt, I realized how I had failed to give and confessed my selfishness. Oh, what little faith I had that day. Didn't God own all the fish of the sea? He could have provided more pins then I could ever imagine, if only I had trusted Him. He certainly had done many miracles in my life in the past. I went to bed forgiven and free but determined I would not miss out on the blessing of giving next time.

Prayer: *"Dear Father, Thank you for not giving up on me when I chose selfishness over Your will. I know I am happiest when I use my gifts of encouraging and giving for You. You are an awesome God and I ask that You continue to use me for Your glory."*

A Cute Little Purse

"Now to him who is able to do immeasurably more than all we ask or imagine, according to his power that is at work within us."

—Ephesians 3:20

My husband and I decided to sell things on eBay to make some extra cash. He would be retiring soon, and we had been exploring ways to make extra giving and fun money. So he said, "Why not give eBay a try?" With that in mind, we took off to a few yard sales to make our first eBay purchases to sell.

It had started to rain, so when we finally arrived at a yard sale, the man had pulled everything into the garage. He said he was done for the day. I made a comment about coming all the way to his sale and he said just take what you want. I looked around and didn't see much of interest. Just as we were deciding to leave, I spotted a cute black-and-white purse. At that point, his wife came out into the garage. I said, "Your husband said to take something, so I wanted to take this cute purse." She said it was okay and then turned to her husband and whispered something in a not-too-friendly voice. I then offered to pay for the purse but the husband said, "No, just take it." I told my husband it was disappointing not to find much at the yard sales, but at least we had a purse that might make a good sale. The rain continued and we decided to go home. I was hoping to make some deals, but in the end, we agreed that yard sales in the rain are not much fun!

We decided to put the purse on eBay and my hubby took a few pictures. We discovered it was a Kate Spade purse and put it up on the auction. What a surprise to have seventy-nine hits and an offer within a few hours. As it turned out, God provided a free purse that we got more than we would ask for and more than we could have imagined. It was a designer purse and in demand. God provided a miracle again!

Prayer: *"Dear Father, Thank you for your wonderful surprise and unexpected blessing by providing a free purse that sold on eBay. I know I can never out give you because you are able to do more than I can even imagine. Thank you for loving me so much!"*

I Don't Have Time for This!

*"I am the LORD, the God of all mankind.
Is anything too hard for me?"*

—Jeremiah 32:27

It was my day off work, and it was beginning to fill up already. I was hoping to sneak in a few "quiet moments" of relaxation and meditation. Things I had to do included exercising at Planet Fitness, grocery shopping, paying bills, cleaning the house, making dinner, doing a load of laundry, going to the post office, and most importantly, picking up an encouraging card for my friend who had cancer. I certainly needed help to get this all done, so I said a quick prayer that morning as I was heading out, "Help me, Lord Jesus, I give this day to you. Help me to see what is really important and make sure I get that done."

A few seconds later, I got a text from a friend who asked me to join her at Panera Bread for coffee and "to talk." She had just retired and needed a listening ear. I felt the Spirit of God lead me and said that I could join her. I drove to Panera and encouraged my friend in the Lord and then continued my to-do list.

I got my errands all done except getting a card for my friend with cancer. As I was leaving Planet Fitness, I thought about how expensive cards are and how much time it would take to find just the right one. I decided to stop at the Rescue Mission Store next door hoping to find one quickly. I searched the store and found not one but two perfect "uplifting" cards. I was running late and wanted to get home to get dinner going as my husband and I had a commitment that night at seven. I went to the cash register to pay and a new clerk asked me how much the cards were. I said I didn't know and she said she would have to call the manager. I thought, "I don't have time for this!" I started getting internally upset. The manager came and asked me where I found the cards. My impatience was climbing from warm to hot, thinking about the time I was wasting. "Doesn't anyone know anything in this store?" I thought. I then took the manager back to where I found the cards. She said that they don't carry individual cards, just packages of cards that are sealed and that she had no idea how the individual cards got there. She told me to just keep them. I couldn't believe it and thanked her profusely. I had gotten two Hallmark cards, which weren't supposed to be there, that had beautiful encouraging thoughts on them, for free! My impatience turned to joy as I realized God had provided another miracle in my life. And to think I almost missed it because of my perceived "time" schedule.

Prayer: *"Dear Father, thank you for once again showing up in my day. You are so awesome and loving. Help me remember my times are in your hands and nothing is too hard for you."*

I Am Right and That's All There Is to It!

"Finally, all of you, be like-minded, be sympathetic, love one another, and be compassionate and humble."

—1 Peter 3:8

 We were going to a "Lifeonaire" conference in the middle of January. We were driving to St. Louis about six hours from where we live. I had been praying three things for my marriage that we could accomplish at that conference:

1. I wanted more humor in our marriage.
2. I wanted to discuss some goals for our future since my husband was retiring soon.
3. And I wanted to spend some quality time alone with my husband.

It was snowing lightly as we headed out that morning, and it was very beautiful. My husband had not really wanted to go, but I had strongly suggested we needed to go and get some direction for our life. I knew I was right and that was all there was to that. We were going!

We had a good breakfast and were drinking coffee in the car as we were driving. We were having a fun time. Then about two hours later, out of nowhere, "a white out" snowstorm appeared on the highway. Traffic came to a stop. We were surrounded by semi-trucks. It was a massive snowstorm and we crept inches at a time. After two hours and having gone only one mile, it was no longer enjoyable. Questions flooded my mind! Why was I so insistent about going in the middle of the winter? I humbly prayed silently asking God to forgive me for my proud spirit and asked Him to help. We began to wonder what was going on ahead of us. Was it a horrific accident? Had someone died? The snow was coming so fast our windshield wipers could not keep up. Plus, you can only imagine how desperately I needed a bathroom after having so much coffee and there were no exits! We were stuck with no escape! After talking with my husband, we decided to have a positive attitude and make the best of it. We started out by counting our blessings and then we began to share what we wanted our future to look like when Steve retired. We were definitely spending quality time together with no interruptions. And after pondering my limited options, we both laughed so hard when I went to the bathroom under a blanket into a coffee mug.

We ended up only going seven miles in five and a half hours. But we were safe and I had gotten my three prayers answered: We found humor, discussed goals for our future, and spent quality time with each other! And I learned to not be so demanding and proud. God had provided once again!

Prayer: *"Dear Father, thank you for providing safety and for the blessing of answered prayers, in spite of my prideful attitude of thinking I was right. Help me to be loving, compassionate, and humble. I know Your way is always right, not mine!"*

I Quit

"But they who wait for the LORD shall renew their strength; they shall mount up with wings like eagles, they shall run and not be weary; they shall walk and not faint."

—Isaiah 40:31

I was at an all-time low. I was very depressed and felt like giving up. I knew God had called me to teach a Ladies' Bible study every other Tuesday night, so why did I feel like a failure. I literally spent hours in preparation and prayer and yet did not see any outward results for my effort and time. I went to prayer asking God . . . or should I say telling God, "I quit!" I had done what He asked me, tried it and failed, so I was quitting. I began to rationalize why I should not have the study: Only three ladies came, no one ever volunteered to have the study at their home, it costs money to buy treats and drinks, *and* my husband had to leave the house or go down in the basement. I felt unappreciated and was tired and saw little growth in the ladies.

I was enjoying my pity party and feeling justified when my dog started barking loudly. The mail had arrived. I went to the mailbox and got the mail. I noticed an envelope with my name on it. I tore it open and began to read the beautiful card. It was a note of appreciation from Susie, stating how much she had grown in the Lord because of God using me as the teacher in our Bible study. She said she had been lost and discouraged and had now found hope and joy. She looked so forward to coming to the Bible study each week and thanked me for being faithful and obedient. Susie closed by saying she wanted to bring treats the following week and would it be okay if she brought a friend.

The tears began to come down my cheeks as I realized it was the Lord's study, not mine, and I needed to wait upon Him and His timing. I confessed my lack of faith, pride, and entitlement. I hugged my dog and felt revived and encouraged. I grabbed my Bible and began to prepare for the next study.

Fast-forward to the present time. We now have twelve ladies attending the Bible study and God has blessed beyond measure in changing lives through His word. And to think I almost quit.

Prayer: *"Dear Father, thank you for renewing my strength, by using Susie's encouraging words when I felt like quitting. Thank you for never giving up on me and providing another miracle in my daily life at just the right moment."*

I Am so Mad

"Do all things without murmurings and disputing."

—Philippians 2:14

I was so tired. It was five days before Christmas, and I still did not have all my shopping done. It was a cold, wintery day as I got out of my car in Penny's parking lot. I walked in the front door, passing the "bell ringer" who was smiling cheerfully. In the store, I headed to the men's department. I was on a mission with my shopping list and a time schedule too! There were so many people, and I couldn't find the shirt I needed for my son-in-law. I became frustrated and then mad. My thoughts became bad; why don't they ever have what I want? The kids better appreciate all I do for them. I finally picked up a shirt and ran over to the long checkout line. I continued with my negative, angry thoughts. Why don't they have more checkout lines; don't they realize it's Christmas time? My mind continued to race as I waited for my turn to pay. I had so much to do for Christmas. By the time I finished paying, I was in a Bah Humbug mood. I exited the door and there was the bell ringer singing joyfully. She had a beautiful voice and the song she was singing. "Away in a Manger" caught me off guard. When she finished, she said, "Hope you are enjoying the season." I suddenly realized I had missed the joy of the day because of my bad attitude. I dug out some change and asked her how long her shift was as she looked cold. She said she had been there twelve hours because the person who was to relieve her never showed up. But she said she didn't mind; she was serving the Lord and she loved it. I thanked her and continued to my car.

I was convinced immediately about the true gifts of the holidays, not presents but God's presence in my life. I saw how my anger had robbed me of the true joy of Christmas. I prayed and confessed my anger and asked God to help me remember the real meaning of Christmas.

Prayer: *"Dear Father, thank you for the example of the bell ringer. Help me to remember the purpose of your birth, the true meaning of Christmas."*

Gate 15

*"I love the LORD because he hath heard
my voice and my supplications."*

—Psalm 116:1

Goodbyes have always been hard for me. I have moved around a lot because of my husband's job, so you would think saying goodbye to friends and family would be easy. I moved eight times in fifteen years, and it seemed to just get harder. Even though saying goodbye was hard, I took every chance I got to spend time with family or friends. Being far away made those relationships that much sweeter. So when I had a chance to meet my daughter in Florida and spend some alone time with her, I was pretty excited. We were going to take a birthday cruise and enjoy the warm weather and reconnect as mother and daughter. She lives in California and would fly to Florida to meet up with me. She did, and we had a wonderful week of adventure and fellowship. I was so thankful for the precious time we had been able to share together.

Our vacation ended, and we went to the airport to go our separate ways to our homes. "If only I could have two more hours at the airport with her," I thought. But we had different flights and time schedules, and I knew this was not possible. I hugged her and held back the tears and proceeded to my departure gate, Gate 15. My flight to Chicago would be leaving in two hours. I bought a soda and then sat down and began to pull a book out of my carry on bag. I started to read, when I heard the words, "Hey, Mom!" I looked up and saw my daughter. She said, "You aren't going to believe this, but I leave out of Gate 15 in three and a half hours." I couldn't believe it. What were the odds of that? God was at work again.

Prayer: *"Dear Father, I love You! Thank you for hearing my unspoken prayer and being so good to me! You are an awesome God and I am so blessed."*

Vanished

"The Lord will guide you always: He will satisfy your needs in a sun-scorched land and will strengthen your frame. You will be like a well-watered garden, like a spring whose waters will never fail."

—Isaiah 58:11

I was exhausted and frustrated as we waited at the airport in San Diego. There were six of us: myself, my husband, son, daughter, and two of their friends, all returning from our eight-day vacation. We had a six-hour wait before we could board our plane and go home. Having gotten up at the crack of dawn, I did not have the desire or the patience to sit in an airport for six more hours. I prayed to God, asking Him to bump us onto an earlier flight. I then headed toward the ticket counter where there was an airline representative. He explained to me that there were only five seats on the flight that would be leaving in an hour. I discussed it with my husband who agreed to take the kids and get home earlier.

I just knew God could provide another seat! I gathered the kids in a circle and prayed for a sixth seat so we could all get home earlier. My daughter's friend, Laura, was testing God to see if He really cared. Her mom and dad, although they were Christians, were getting a divorce and Laura was hurting. I continued to pray silently asking God to do a miracle and encourage Laura and me by showing His power in providing another seat.

Well, the five of them boarded the plane ten minutes later as I sat nearby waving goodbye. I was physically exhausted and emotionally drained and just wanted to go home. After everyone got on the plane, the airline worker began counting the tickets. I went up one last time and asked if there was a no-show. He said no, every seat was filled. He continued to count the tickets then looked up at me and said, "I need to count these again, someone disappeared." He counted again and then made a phone call to the stewardess on the plane. A few minutes later he said, "I don't understand this, but there is one seat available on the plane, go and get it." I ran to the gate, boarded the plane, and saw an empty seat that was right beside my husband. I couldn't believe it! Laura saw me and shrieked with joy.

God knew my physical and mental need. He had answered my prayer and encouraged the rest of the family. What a wonderful way to end our vacation.

Prayer: *"Dear Father, thank you for caring for my needs, for answering my prayer, and for showing your power through it."*

I Will Give Joyfully

"Each one of you should give as you have decided in your heart to give. You should not be sad when you give, and you should not give because you feel forced to give. God loves the person who gives happily."

—2 Corinthians 9:7

I had just heard a Bible lesson on giving, and I was excited to try it out. It was a cold Thursday morning and my husband and I were going out to eat breakfast. As we were standing in line to order, I was being "alert" to see how I could treat someone without them knowing it. Out of nowhere, a man walked up to me and handed me a gift card for my meal. I started to say "No, thanks" but he was gone in a flash. I was shocked but my husband said just take it. We enjoyed our free meal and headed to the mall. I needed to buy a present for my four-year-old nephew. I had got him a cameo shirt but wanted to buy him a toy too. He loved "Jake the pirate." I looked at the Jake toys, but they were out of my budget. I moved to the clearance section and looked at cars and trucks but still hoped for a Jake toy. I glanced at a large ball and then I saw it, right behind the ball, Jake the pirate ship 45 percent off. It was the right price, in my budget. I couldn't believe it. God had given me two gifts that day when I was looking for some stranger to give too.

Next we went to the movie theater for our weekly date. As we were in line to buy our tickets, I realized I forgot our refillable popcorn bucket. I paid for the tickets and the lady said, "You have free popcorn coming today." I was overwhelmed at God's goodness and gifts for me. I was willing to obey and give, and he had once again showed me his love for me.

Prayer: *"Dear Father, thank you for showing me that I can never out give you. Help me to obey and be willing to give out of my heart cheerfully. Thank you once again for performing three miracles in my life on that cold Thursday."*

Sell That House

"Great is the Lord and most worthy of praise.
His greatness no one can fathom."

—Psalm 145:3

I was enjoying a wonderful visit with my adult son in our hot tub. After laughing and joking, I became more serious and asked him if he had any prayer requests.

"Mom, please pray for our house in Ohio to sell," he said. He had moved three years ago and was making two house payments. Renters came and left and the last renter had made a "mess "of the home.

I had prayed off and on for the past three years for his ranch home to sell. But I was determined to pray without ceasing for the next two weeks. I begged and pleaded with God to "sell their home." I praised God for his power and ability to do all things, even sell their home, which was the nicest home on the block but in a bad area. It became number one on my prayer list. I claimed scripture that said, "Nothing is too hard for you God and all things are possible with you."

But I was still shocked and surprised when "the call" came five days later from my son. "Mom, you are not going to believe this. We got a cash offer on our house in Ohio and we have to close this week." I was overwhelmed with God's goodness and his fast answer to my prayers. I couldn't have dreamed of a cash offer and closing in a week.

Prayer: *"Dear Father, you are so worthy of praise and goodness. Thank you for answering my prayer above and beyond what I could even have imaged. Thank you, Lord, for showing up and doing a miracle once again in my life."*

Peace Is Overrated

"Now may the Lord of peace himself give you peace at all times and in every way. The Lord be with you all."

—2 Thessalonians 3:16

Everyone was concerned about Joni. She had stage 3 cancer, and at her last checkup, she had not improved at all. Joni was new to our women's Bible study but all ten of us gals loved her immediately. She was kind and shy but also anxious. The girls were concerned because she had no peace about her health and life. One of the gals, Judy, said, "We need a miracle and I know God can perform it." So the ladies agreed and gathered around Joni and we laid hands on her and prayed. As the weeks passed and Joni continued to decline, we prayed all the more. As the Christmas season approached, Joni missed our Bible study due to her chemo treatments, but the ladies were faithful in their prayers for her. Another gal, Barb, mentioned she wished Joni had more peace. Flipidly, I said, "Peace is overrated and she is a believer and God can handle her. Let's just continue to pray for her."

A few days later, the Holy Spirit spoke to me and said, "Go see Joni." It was an extremely busy day for me, and I tried to ignore the urge. I argued, saying I had so much to do being a few days before Christmas, like baking, gift wrapping, and cooking favorite foods.

"And, Lord, she lives so far away." But I had no peace as I was convicted to go and visit her and I eventually gave in and drove forty-five minutes to her home.

As I visited with Joni, she shared all that had been going on and it was not good news. The cancer had spread. She was very anxious and heavy hearted. As I listened and offered hope through Jesus, she became quiet and thoughtful. She had never asked Jesus to save her and become her personal savior. She said she always knew there was a God somewhere out there. She said she wanted to know Jesus on a more personal level, and right there in her living room, surrounded by her dogs, she opened her heart to Jesus. That moment, the miracle of peace occurred and Joni's face showed it. After hugging her and sharing tears of Joy, I left praising God. I would never say peace was overrated again and would continue to look to the Lord for direction and my peace.

Prayer: *"Dear Father, thank you for saving Joni and giving her your lasting peace for now and for eternity. And thank you for teaching me to obey your voice and to always listen to the Holy Spirit and seek your peace."*

About the Author

Shirlee R. Mooney is a lifelong Bible student, popular Bible teacher, and published freelance writer. She's also a retired hospice nurse, business owner, beach lover, and chocolate addict.

As the mother of two grown children and grandma to two beautiful grandbabies (Arrow and Pierce), she is kept busy traveling and enjoying creating memories with her family.

Shirlee lives with her husband, Steve, in Michigan along with her cat, Tiki, and her psycho-dog, Bently.

CPSIA information can be obtained
at www.ICGtesting.com
Printed in the USA
FSHW022048240621
82609FS